THE WATER LEVELING
WITH US

DONALD LEVERING

RED MOUNTAIN PRESS

The author is grateful to the editors of these publications, in which the following poems first appeared: *The Alembic*, "Explain To Me About Plums," "Live from the Airbus Belly Camera"; *Central Avenue*, "The Black Madonna"; *Chelonian Conservation and Biology*, "A Need"; *The Drunken Boat*, "The Other Half"; *Hunger Mountain*, "Counting for the Apparition of William Stafford"; *Iron Horse Literary Review*, "Man Leads Whooping Cranes Through Lost Migration Route"; *Poets For Living Waters*, "Lines Written Under 13,000 Pounds Per Square Inch"; *Sin Fronteras/Writers Without Borders*, "What We Last Saw"; *Stirring*, "Last Will & Testament"; and *Together Yes*, "The Water Leveling With Us."

ISBN 978-0-9855031-6-1

Printed in the United States of America

RED MOUNTAIN PRESS
Santa Fe, New Mexico
www.redmountainpress.us

To Lois May

Contents

I

ALL THEY HAVE TO LEARN

The children born upon the hill
have never had to puzzle where
their fruit is from   it rolls before
their doors and down the hill   papaya
orange grapefruit lemon   always
rolling by their feet   they never
have to climb for mango grapefruit
lime   never shake a tree
the wind and time undo the fruit
          and all the children have to do
is learn the knack of reaching down
to grab the rolling fruit   and not
to raise to mouth the ones that are
at rest   they're split from falling hard
and black with swarming ants
          and apples sprayed to never age
are shipped from somewhere cold and dumped
to roll into the marketplace
          they're bruised   the children's daddies bag
bananas green to wheel away
to boats   the girls are barely more
than girls when bellies swell with children
to be born upon the hill   that crawls
with men in trucks that haul the fruit   the trees away

Howler Monkeys

Unlike capuchins,
who cadge for handouts
and bare their teeth while reaching,

howlers stay in the rainforest.
If we spot them, they're way up in the branches,
remote from jaguars

and from us.
Through scopes we see they're grooming
or cracking open nuts.

At dusk their voices come
from someplace deep in the forest,
fearsome growls that swell

to loud bravado, even booming,
not quite human,
not quite not.

The Black Madonna

of St. Jacques Cathedral stares
from an altarpiece painting.
Her eyes, dark as well water,
gather mica flakes
as Sofía dusts the candlesticks.

She hears the bishop's wheezing
as he nears. He must suffer
from the dust, Sofía thinks,
but why from the belfry does she see
such gusts of dust ascending?

Her eyes rest on Candomblé women
on the graveyard path below
offering to passers-by charmed vipers.

In the market she learns it was the first
tremor that birthed the rising dust.
The second blurred her face in the well
and rang the basilica's bells.
The third shock spilled a trainload of coal.

The cathedral clock is stopped.
The churchyard gate won't latch.
Within the walls are people camped
in tents of smoke. *Why are they stealing
candles from the church?*, the bishop asks.

Sofía leaves the painted Black Madonna
collecting dust, follows the Candomblé girls,
places candles on the graveyard path.

AFTER COUNTING QUEEN CONCHS

Shimmering pixels on the surface
as swallows bank and titter
over calm seas in low sun

Fish flopping under the dock
punctuate the quiet dusk
One blue heron stalks the strand

Three barefoot girls
begin to softly sing

> *This old man, he played one,*
> *He played knick-knack on my thumb*

Today we dove to ocean floor
to search for queen conchs
to add to the scientists' census

Other islands are heaped with middens
of their pierced shells
They were thought to be innumerable

Dangling legs from the dock
the dark sisters continue

> *This old man, he played two,*
> *He played knick-knack on my shoe*

A NEED

Playa Grande, Costa Rica

From dark waters she emerges
at night heavy with eggs
Breathing hard,
she drags her seven hundred pounds
up the beach, flippers churning sand
inching her way uphill

We who witness her massive apparition
of the deep come to land,
her dogged struggle, her need,
stand amidst a hatchery of stars

≈   ≈   ≈

A wide track of darkened sand leads
                to the zenith of her climb
where she digs her body pit,
flailing sand in all directions,
disguising her nesting chamber's site,
which she now scoops out with her back flippers,
precise flippersful of wet sand lifted
                and placed to the side
        of the meter-deep chamber
where the future of her kind will incubate

≈   ≈   ≈

Might this be the last beach
where this ancient turtle lays her eggs
Will she who cannot live in captivity,
she who has survived
earthquakes and tsunamis,
meteorites and ice ages,

be snuffed by the big-brained ape,
stealing her eggs,
drowning her in fishing nets,
turning her night-nesting beaches
into bright playgrounds,
frightening her back to sea

≈   ≈   ≈

A need
for undeveloped beaches of imagination,
        dark pits of potential

A need to know that somewhere in the Gulf
of Papagayo or the deep Pacific,
in the Atlantic or Indian oceans,
huge reptiles are swimming
feeding   mating   migrating

A need to believe that generations hence
leatherbacks will still be grazing on jellyfish,
that the largest sea turtle in the world, rife with eggs,
will still swim toward dark beaches

≈   ≈   ≈

Which of the eggs
she has just laid
will hatch
Which hatchlings will escape raccoons
crabs   gulls   dogs   monkeys   humans
and skitter into the sea

The mother covers up the answers,
wheels her enormous bulk
back toward the black water,
edges down the slope,
finally reaches wet sand,
rests,
waiting for a wave to lift her.

Afloat at last, she paddles,

                    disappears

EXPLAIN TO ME ABOUT PLUMS

Venid a ver la sangre por las calles.
                    — from "Explico Algunas Cosas"

Come to me, Pablo,
explain about ripe plums,
how their sweet juice redeems
even the junta that tried to silence you.

With juice of a plum
would you paint for me
the light leaking through blindfolds?
Tell me how these plums tasted so sweet
in the same city where human blood
ran in the streets.

Hymns for the dispossessed
swell in your poems, sweat
of peasants inks the pages.
Ambassador of Avocados,
would you return to your senators
to scold once more,

> *Not only is famine lack of bread,*
> *but also hoarding of land.*

Diplomat of the Pacific, speak to me
about those washed-up figureheads
you retrieved from the strand to your home.
Did they keen about the sea worms
gnawing your nation's democracy,
did they moan of the undertow
dragging your people below?

When the colonels tried to gag you,
Neruda, they did not realize,
as they crossed off names on their lists,
that each victim's disappearance
multiplied your poems' tongues.

But what I want to know, Señor Plum,
is how did you stuff newspapers
between your skin and your shirt
and not get stained with impermanence?

Let me follow you, Official of Odes,
ambling through the market,
palming apples in your hands,
or blowing saxophone riffs on a breadfruit.

Tell me, my bald Chilean Whitman,
when you were eyeing gardenias,
or whimsically naming the beasts,
or lolling on the beach,
could you ever forget
the blood running in the streets?

THE CALCIUM OF STARS

> *Those who have a memory are able to live in this*
> *fragile present moment; those who have none*
> *don't live anywhere.*
> — *Patricio Guzmán, "Nostalgia for the Light"*

Driest desert on earth, the Atacama
Sun sears it throughout the year
Lichens survive on fog blown in from sea

From the coast the Atacama rises
thousands of meters to a ridge
where radio telescopes
listen for the stars' first stories.
Astronomers chart each surfacing star's
calcium thumbprint

Below the telescope towers,
anything discarded desiccates
Hard minerals, shells, and bones—remain

Memory is rock and crevice

      ≈   ≈   ≈

Down on the bleaching plains
female forms stoop
to peer like soothsayers into rocks
They are not prospecting for copper
Not breathing life back into the ruins
of workers' camps for mining saltpeter
Not picking through tailings for silver

These women are digging into desert
raising the whitest stones
to find their loved ones' remains

Each of whom on a certain day
that began as any other
in the reign of Augusto Pinochet

disappeared

≈   ≈   ≈

Miners believe in the luck
bestowed by *los alicantos*,
giant birds of the Atacama

It is said they nest in hidden caves
devouring shiny ores
and may be glimpsed at night
flying over mining camps,
their wings glittering metallic hues,
their eyes emitting eerie light

To follow an *alicanto*
is to find the mother lode of silver
or richest vein of gold

But with its dazzling wings and eyes
the bird mesmerizes searchers
and leads them into abyss

≈   ≈   ≈

The bones of *los desaparecidos,*
"the disappeared," wizened
by sun and wind, remain
for their stories to be told

One captive drew an exact floor plan
of the Atacama prison camp

He'd paced it off,
scratched figures on scraps,
stashed it all in memory,
and buried himself in the garbage
to escape with torture's map

Others, those husbands, sons, and brothers
of the women who probe the desert,
were disposed of, quickly covered over
with a scattering of pebbles and sand

But nothing stays forever buried
Somewhere in the Atacama
pieces of *los desaparecidos*
will wait until the stars expire

≈   ≈   ≈

Absent moisture, a body does not rot
Its genetic badge persists within
the calcium of its teeth and bones
to be matched with surviving kin

One leather-skinned seeker
hears her husband's ghost
prowling within gritty gusts

Another of the missing's sister
delving through a crack
is startled by an *alicanto*
sparkling in its nest

A third woman affirms she will turn over
every pebble in the Atacama
until she finds the rubble of her son

> *I wish the telescopes*
> *didn't just scan the sky,*
> *but also listened into earth*

II

As the President Rallies the Nation

On the other side of the planet,
in that poppy-growing land
the president wants us to bomb,
a mouse is napping.

We're supposed to be on his side,
so we leave the TV on as we bring
our water glasses with us to the lawn.
While he stokes fear in millions of rooms,

we're peering at the cratered moon.
To hold the view, our backyard telescope
adjusts for earth's rotation.
A little motor keeps the focus trained
on the gray and silver Sea of Ingenuity.

The motor whirs a small sound
like the dozing mouse's breathing
a world away.

Through the window in our living room,
the frowning TV figure
raises his right arm to point a finger.
From out here he looks very small.

Over where the mouse is snoozing,
morning breezes wave through papery blooms.

And the moon continues to sway
every water molecule
in oceans and heartlands,
as it eases in and out of view.

WAR TAXES

We are herded into the junior high school gym,
ordered to roll up our sleeves
to donate blood to the giant

who is leaking oil
from the back of his head
down to a puddle.

At the front of the line, several
are hooked up to the shunt
into the giant's groin.

Face gone white, the boy
beside me buckles.
A private arrives with mop and pail.

WORDS FROM THE WOODS

Words had less currency than faces and hands for
knowing whom I could trust — Aharon Appelfeld

A table heaped with goose feathers —
my mother and aunts around it
stuffing feathers into bedding.

Uncle Harmon in his frayed yarmulke
noodling his button accordion.
Papa with his book in the overstuffed chair.

How they all shone in the candlelight.

Our house smelled of apples baking.
A knock came to the door.
An officer read a proclamation.

It was the last I saw my mother.

They had run out of boxcars
so they marched us to the camp.
Nine days of blisters and thirst.

They put me with skeleton children.
Papa's last words—*Don't talk.*
Watch how things are done.

I was ten. How I escaped
I will not say. No telling when
I may need to do it again.

Wandering forests and farms
I lived on mushrooms and bugs
and scraps I begged from peasants,
using signs, pretending to be mute.

Hidden in the woods I counted
train cars passing, I counted heads.
In the dark I counted crusts of bread.

Two years I was friends with forest animals
and stranger to men.

Once I came on a pumpkin burst in the road.
The pulp was mashed into mud.
But I retrieved hundreds of seeds
and toasted them on a scrap of tin.

Little Fire was my friend.

Little Fire, and a silver fox
who shared my feast of seeds,
neither thinking it odd.

For wasn't I the only person shivering
that night in the bog by the river
when the frogs began?

Chirping, croaking, blatting,
and big ones were booming
while peepers were tooting,

and all were moving to the river.

This entire spectacle
for me alone, and heedless of me,
they hopped past by the hundreds.

And wasn't I twice-blessed
to be frightened into a sweat
by the giant stag standing on hind feet,
head tilted so his antlers seemed like a crown?
He didn't speak, yet he did,

words from the woods before words.

SALT STONES

Where I am can not be told
so I am elsewhere

> *Sprinkling salt on boulders*
> *for the sheep to lick*
> *How smooth those stones become*

They want me to say names and places

> *Among cloud trees blooming*
> *over the school's rocky soccer field*

They offer names to betray

> *The blame is to be found within*

I ask to speak to a lawyer
Laughter—"Where do you think you are?"

> *I lie down to hide from my brother*
> *I listen to the blurry call for prayers*

The rubber disc is smacked on my scrotum
A wire leads to the power

> *How did they get my daughter's picture*

A doctor is brought in —
"On a scale from one to ten..."

    Thousands of bees buzzing
    in the poppy field

They seize my scripture
They piss on it

    I want to bite off their pricks

One asks the other to help
fasten me to waterboard

    Raindrops bounce off boulders

The other bends to help tighten
Their hands lightly brush each other's skin

    How I love to rub my hands
    over those tongue-smoothed stones
    then through oily wool

They demand to know who and where
They can not be told

    The sheep are known by a handful of names

The Other Half

I was bringing back firewood ...

This isn't half the story.
The other half is one sandal print

between two dents in dust.

The other half are cities of mismatched crutches.
The other half are called *los mutilados*.

The other half cannot forget fragments

of metal and stones,
of dirt, muscle and bone,

and pieces of the other sandal

blown into the bloodstream.
The other leg is blackened

and smells of gangrene.

I was on my way to the well ...
The other story is how they were sown

in fields like potatoes.

I was on my way to make charcoal ...
The other side is about pain.

Of how they were hidden in bridges and roads.

I was going to dig for cassava ...
The other half is the missing map

of placements.

The other half of the field
is fenced off.

I was fetching a cow that had wandered off ...

LIVE FROM THE AIRBUS BELLY CAMERA

Through the seat-back screen
the silent seascape scrolls—
mammoth icebergs reduced
to thumbnail moons,
ships with their crews and freight
mere blips recalling news clips

of factories and bridges disappearing
in soundless puffs of our prior wars.
Weighing more than three blue whales,
our craft courses breakneck through the sky;
its shadow overtakes the coast of Iceland.
To background engine hum

fjords and forests roll under the belly cam.
Black chasms and glacier-cloaked volcanoes
pass; the drama below, obscured
by scattered cirrus scrim, presumed
to still include the polar bear and caribou
among the crunching snowmobiles.

Across the aisle a boy has slid
his window blind; his handheld toy
booms with ersatz war
intruding on our buzzing ambience
before earphones seal him in
with his detonating thumbs.

Behind cramped trays of drinks and food,
we change the seat-back screen to news—
an air strike witness posts
pictures of a charred street car
and cycling paperboy caught fire.
In the liquor and lull of airplane thrum,

we cruise above and far removed.

VIEWS OF A DRONE PILOT

With my feet down deep in Cheyenne Mountain
I've been watching Omar for seven weeks
through relays from a satellite parked above his town

I log the patterns of his life —
walking to homes of family and cohorts,
trips to market, mornings to mosque

In infrared I view Omar's roof
where summer nights he beds with his wife
How odd it makes me feel

     when their crimson fields fuse

Still, I do not hesitate when the order comes,
but my target is hard to isolate
so there are collaterals

I view the funeral
Count bodies carried out of the house
I can't not see the women flail

     and raise their faces to the sky

III

Pictures from the Permafrost

In this satellite image, a landscape of thawing permafrost appears like a section of white and gray bone, full of openings. —U.S. *Geological Survey*

Nine months no one can dig.
The newly dead remain unburied.
Waste stays frozen.

Nights bent to scrimshaw.
To mending snowshoes and mittens.
Nights given over to drum song
before the satellite dish.

≈   ≈   ≈

In the season of frenzied flies
a bereaved family digs and buries.
Others gather salmonberries.

An airplane growls to ground.
A man and his wife step out
to capture photographs.

In spongy soil their tent stakes will not grip.
They scout about the strip
and find a cannibalized Beechcraft.
Inside they mate and roll into sleep.

≈   ≈   ≈

When tundra thaws
objects surge from below.
This story is familiar, but
now the permafrost is thawing.

What had been buried in seal season
deep enough to stay beneath
with haunting dreams
is pushing up and out.

Plastic packaging. Dead batteries.
Even whalebone foundations
from long abandoned homes
heave up through the slush.

≈   ≈   ≈

The journalist focuses
on an unearthed humpback's skull.
Her camera isolates a fluke bone.
Petrol can. Vodka bottle.
Cracked snowshoe. The shutter snaps.

≈   ≈   ≈

All the dogs and people
gather to share the bull walrus
being butchered on shore.
The birds of summer circle.

Offerings of cheeks and heart.
Carving knives and laughter.
Smacking lips, camera clicks.

≈   ≈   ≈

Sledding back to everlasting night.
Back to stories of stalking bear
and the dog that lost its courage.

Stories of a witch girl with white hair
and the trackless trek to the land of ghosts
before the clamor of the drilling rig.

Before its incandescence
swallowed Little Bear.

≈   ≈   ≈

Human bones are surfacing
from boggy ground.
Rib cage. Backbone. Femur.
Little pelvis.

Elders recall the plague
that killed with spots and fever.
The village almost whited-out.

One extended dusk exposure
frames a snowy owl
perched upon a risen skull.

The crimson seedcracker is back.
A stalk of red oat grass bends
with her weight. Grass
has been growing back
since wildebeests and cattle
were fenced off.
Grasses thick and tall.

Acacia saplings are back. Candelabrums too.
Dominions of cooling shade expand.

Inside the fence that keeps out people
and their cattle, where land mines are planted,
they're back.
Ticks in tall grass, swarming gnats.
The quick-tongued sand snake,
black beetles that it snags.

Cattle trails grown over. Wheel ruts filling up.
A white-eared barbet whistles atop a baobab.
A grasshopper is caught mid-air by a bustard.

Termites move the mines away from their nest
without tripping them. Guinea fowl
scurry through thickets on light feet.
The tiny aardwolf does not explode.

But the mongoose in pursuit
digs hard and quick.

PREPARE

It all begins with rain
How it keeps pouring down
The people all huddled round

TVs plugged into the Everlasting
Radios tuned to The Great Beyond
And the news is bigger than anything we've known

The rain keeps coming down
Pours off roofs rises in streets
Climbs levees of Lake Pontchartrain

Wind is throwing big limbs down
Frogs stop croaking birds fold tight
Animals march to higher ground
The rain keeps coming down

Then a woman on radio says
        People Prepare
And everybody thinks she's talking about the rain
Thinks she means we better gather our belongings

But the woman goes on saying
        Train's a-comin' It's on its way
Though we can hardly hear her for the storm
Knocking trees down clogging drains

Now water rises over porches
Branches break window panes
And the woman on radio is crowing
How proud she is to be the preacher
Of the Church of Lake Pontchartrain

Says her congregation have catfish humming hymns
Says they teach crawfish how to pray
Says her net for catching souls for Jesus
            is wide as her voice on radio waves

And the man who's telling you this story
He sees water climbing up his stoop
Has to leave his cats behind

Has to leave his banjo and his books
Let them soak in muddy dirge
Has to rush to cram his car
Pile in his wife and crying daughters

And the preacher is shouting
            Ah don't care about the rain
            Ah don't mind the wind
            Ah will visit every parishioner every fish
            Ah will teach 'em all about the Rapture

Loaded cars snake out of town
Catfish big as pigs swim in the streets
Over by the levee people wave from their roofs
Rain keeps coming down

It isn't only water rushing over levees
It's 'gators eating lapdogs
Children scared by hairy men
And bloated house cats floating past

            Here comes little Moses drifting in a basket
            There in waist deep water stands The Baptist

There's a house of old folks waiting for their saviors
And water keeps on rising keeps on rising

Roads wash out—people leaves their cars
Long trains of folks with soggy shoes

Still comes the voice of Pontchartrain
>   *Why you worryin' what's blowin' down*
>   *Why you frettin' what's washin' away*
>   *Now's the time to welcome Rapture*

If we raise our arms in praise, she hollered,
The Righteous will be lifted up
We will ignore our cold wet clothes
Forget our thirst and hunger

>   *Relinquish earthly plans*
>   *Time for the Doomsday Jubilee*
>   *Catfish will be singin' alligators laughin'*

LAST WILL & TESTAMENT

> *And to myself? I offer only the crooked*
> *grin of the toad — Lawrence Durrell*

To the future, I give the rind of the past,
    the dented stone from kneeling knees
    in the floor of Chartres Cathedral,
    the question mark of a staircase
    amid Haitian earthquake rubble.

To History, plucked lute notes
    of eleventh century troubadours
    floating past footprints on the moon.

To Plato I give back the breath that was his.
To poetry I leave behind the obsessive sestina.

To the wounded of Gettysburg,
    Walt Whitman reading letters from home.

To refugees, my good blucher boots.

To the Redeemer, permission to forgive himself
    for letting the dead sleep another century.

To the anxious I give my wristwatch.
To the well-intentioned, *The Hesitation Blues.*

To raven, brass chess pieces,
    smashed aluminum cans,
    the deed to the Kingdom of Language.

To the United States I leave Old Glories
    bankers wiped their hands on.

Science gets Watson's dream
        of the double-helix,
Art inherits Picasso's love-bed scents.

To the Black Madonna's womb,
        I bequeath semen of the Irish elk,
        eggs of the last tree frog.

To the sewers, excrement
        of seven billion souls.
To fields of praise, tulip bulbs.

To fathers and mothers, portraits
        of their fathers and mothers.

To the mirrors, facing mirrors
        and dreams imprisoned within.

To prisoners go my thumbstained copies
        of Shakespeare.

To the new year, old pornographic calendars.
To the old habits, their fears.

To the fashionable I leave my hemline.
To the insincere, the headache of holding a smile.

To musicians, I give the theme of the fugue
        to repeat, I give to their knees
        reverberations from my taiko drum.

To lovers, I offer ears that are deaf to prophecy.

LINES WRITTEN UNDER 13,000 POUNDS PER SQUARE INCH

Deepwater Horizon Spill

Ink from within plumes through mile-deep water,
festoons reeds and corals, turtles and birds
with iridescent pearls of smotheration.

Under such pressure one ink tentacle escapes
the gravity of glued pelicans
to pen my dream of the looping biplane

brought down by a host of monarchs.
How they soften the landing
on the marsh lacquered by the black tide.

Another indigo stream dilutes into
shimmer of fishes weaving through
swaying kelp forests, wave after wave

of lavender anthias, schools of dappled
wrasse, flatfaced tang, damsels
darting their yellows, electric blues.

Viscousness wells under all this.

I dip a brush of cougar's tail
in the gushing pool to paint the shirt
for the reborn Ghost Dance:

>stripes around the wailing throat,
>bluebirds at the breast,
>bows & arrows arcing over shoulders,
>black bison on the back,
>down the leggings lightning snakes,
>blueshifting pigment of dusk
>>smeared on cheekbones,

>black crescent moon forehead trance tattoo.

THE WATER LEVELING WITH US

Polar ice caps may be melting, world war-sized
hurricanes homing in on Manhattan,
but here in Cobscook Bay the tide recedes,
exposes rocks and barnacles, mussels and sea grass;
empties grottoes, bridges islands, dries up
mudflats, draws clammers and scavengers,

among them ravens who assert their corvid
corporate rights over the bared expanse;
they argue with gulls, drive away raccoons,
gang up on sea eagles.

So all the liquid drained from seashores here
fills fjords and coves in distant latitudes,
the moon's means for formulating perfect
equanimity on earth.

Tell that to villages submerged under cubic
miles of sluggish reservoirs; console
the bleaching corals with a mermaid serenade
of tidal charts. To idled fishing fleets, speak
the even-handedness of ocean waves,
the necessary leveling of cod stocks.

Praise the grace of Handel's *Water Music*
to the turtle searching for the nest the rising water
washed away. To seasick refugees in leaky boats,
tout the bounty of plastic flotsam continents.
To all who thirst, preach the gospel of avenging seas.

IV

REVERBERATION

A springtime revolution like shouting tulips
above the ticker scrolling soccer scores
in the lounge where we are reading lips,

drinking inside the woofers of recorded music.
I scribble on a cocktail napkin
The sounds have slipped within.

All consult their palm-held oracles
to open the story going viral
of some poor soul's cerebral tumor,
almost the size of an elephant's ear.

We order more, glancing up.
The witness' mobile clip of upraised fists
repeats like wind-blown spores.

≈   ≈   ≈

My brother and I lower a double bass into
a hole we have dug in my back yard.
No dirge's ostinato, the shovelfuls of dropping
dirt are absent little thumps.

It must be written some place,
The tuning fork at creation's core
no longer reverberates to the hummingbirds.

Missing more than grandstand roar are simple cues—
crisp slipping of paper into envelope, the drag of spoon
across soup pan, the gush of an old bouquet's
rank fluid down a drain.

Fish behind the glass mouth words for our condition.
We gesture, point to overloaded circuits, blasted amps,
cracked tweeters. Soundlessly we stamp our feet
like rhinos gone extinct.

≈　　　≈　　　≈

Camera lamps bleach shadows
from the ceiling of the cave
whose long-eared bats have been

decimated by a snowy fungus.
Close-up of their hanging faces
powdered with white fuzz.

Shots of other caverns
emptied of the rustle
and thrum of bats.

Summer nights without their squeak and flutter.

≈　　　≈　　　≈

Throughway breezes undulate ghost leaves
without a swish or rustle.
Wheeling tractor-trailers sound like nothing.

In a swarm of upraised dust, a medivac
helicopter lands, quiet as a butterfly,
as if the scene were muted on TV.

Everyone is checking power plugs,
yanking out earbuds, texting like crazy.
We cannot fathom where the sounds have fled.

≈   ≈   ≈

Out of cellular range, you parallel a stream.
Each small fall of water lets go its local plash,
the glottal passage over pebbles dropping into pockets

and shushing over bedrock shelf, reverberation
of the gurgle humming off the walls of shale.
Where water widens into bog, you happen on

a caucus of hundreds of blatting bullfrogs.
The tiny bones of your inner ear,
the large ones—breastbone, femur;

the small caverns of your sinuses;
the channels of your four humors—
all are ringing, all resound

with frog song. They synchronize
the oscillation of their din,
and you are rapt inside their pulse.

His great hairless head
indented with a surgical scar
His guileless grin

Happy to meet you

He's glad for each moment
unfettered to any other
Fat baby man   child Buddha

Happy to meet you

His headache
dogged companion
before he went under the knife

is gone

along with all that's transpired
since he returned from the ether
May Day, 1962

What did you say happened to JFK?

Each trip to the church is his first
He has no sins to confess
He passes the Virgin exclaiming again

Her robe — such a shade of blue!

Above the museum door
he encounters words
as if never read before

> *A PEOPLE WHO FORGET THEIR HISTORY*
> *ARE DOOMED TO REPEAT …*

He hasn't a worry within
viewing again as if never before
the bog man preserved in peat

> *… undigested grains of wheat*
> *still in his stomach …*
> *ambush wound in his skull …*

He asks the attendant
exactly the same question
he has asked before

What happened to the poor man's head?

Her answer is instantly gone
along with his question
He extends his hand with a friendly grin

Happy to meet you

and asks once more

What did you say happened to JFK?

WHAT WE LAST SAW

Tell us what you saw
   I was waiting for the light to change
   looking straight into that red mouth
   Everything became the same
   People honking and shouting at me

      In a hurry to return to work
      I was on the elevator
      Pressing the button for my floor
      Now I see nothing but numbers

Are the numbers white on black or black on white
   They are all blank faces

      They are the lottery of rotten luck

      The genome of the final virus

What did you hear
      On radio the president
      trying to sound brave
      about our war
      The station went dead

No one saw it coming
      I was in bed with someone
      not seeing anything
         but the inside of my pleasure
      when it all became gray

So your blindness is gray
>My blindness is flying within fog

>My grayness is unbleached wool

>Mine is the underside of shoe soles

>Ashes of charcoal

What about the rest of us
>I was trying to decide which to buy
>Then there was no difference in anything

Is anyone here not blind
>Some stars had broken up
>in the checkout line magazine
>when I told the stranger beside me
>I'd just gone blind
>But I still can see

You are lying
>I see the flooded deltas behind my eyelids

>The ghosts of panthers loping

>I hear the white rhino
>shuffling in the sawdust of the zoo

What do you feel
>I feel ironic smiles
>flicker on the voices of the blind

COUNTING FOR THE APPARITION OF WILLIAM STAFFORD

One

On evening news the handstanding bridegroom
has flipped from the ferryboat's railing
into the realm of wounded manatees
and never surfaced, the panicked cries
of the wedding guests unheard
inside the river's gloom,
down where *the disappeared*
hold their breath for the count of ten,
and then do their lives over again.

Two

The television counts to itself
all night in the lobby I pass through
on my way to meet the shade
of William Stafford, lingering
by a tree-lined city creek.
Leaves swish past our shoes.
The stream where he appears
has come through the forty year
underground coal mine fires,
from the fractured aquifers
of Kansas, past falling songbirds.

Three

The acreage of logged forests,
the declining tally of barn-door skates
tangled in gill nets, the shrinking number
of tiger preserves, the total of rhino horns
in a mound man-high, the sum of kestrels
killed in the spill, the dwindling
leatherback turtle census, the count
of salmon ascending the ladder, the blur
of animal icons spun in a slot machine.

Four

From a storm of quarks
beside me at the urinals
manifests a self-effacing man
with mild, brown eyes
and perfect poetic pitch
who hums a tune to himself.

I would love to be lulled but
have to look up the monk
whose penance was to inscribe
Eleven Deadly Sins on the heads
of seven dozen pins.
I must click the link to the Black Sox
who threw the World Series
for a shoebox full of crisp bills.

Must stare at the stream of celebrities
grinning on screen, share in the pulse
of a nation of shamechasers,
become one of the numberless motes
of cosmic and commercial dust
exposed by the searchlight
for the used car sale.

Something in William's humming
brings back my dream—
an Irish elk was pleading in Gaelic.

Five

William Stafford's image
among the Douglas firs
implies with a glance
perhaps I should count
falling leaves, or note
propeller scars on manatees,
or travel the aural labyrinth
of a beached porpoise.
Of his deer who died of headlights
or his bomb test lizard
that gripped the quaking desert
what more can be recounted?

Stafford's shade declines to say
whether I should be clicking
on my abacus of grief
the number of butterflies
in an acre of torched rainforest,
or reckoning desperation
in the eyes of the orangutan.
When I ask whether I should be naming
the masks of avarice
or counting whooping cranes,
William's apparition
gives a wry smile.

V

LATE SPRING TWILIGHT

keeps me reading on the porch
as moths trapped indoors bat the glass.
Deep into evening I absorb the report
that won't permit sleep, brooding

over the golden coin turtle
speared through its shell with a litter stick
to save some poacher the effort of stooping.

And this is only one among truckloads
of smuggled turtles, some not yet dead
in Hong Kong heat, released by police
to the rescue team, who bring them

to the sanctuary, where the hopeless
are eased into death. A few survive
to stay forever in cages
safe from poachers.

Have I overexposed this scene?
Shrunk creation to a stage
for villains and heroes to repeat their roles
under klieg lights of outrage?

Pictured a world as color-bleached
as the masses of moribund coral reefs?

Am I one more large-eyed moth
intoxicated with Earth's dire news,
fervid to fly into setting sun?

Fox Farmer's Wife

Oye, Norway

Even with our hundreds, we take care
to keep the kits together with their mothers
in the same cages. Besides,
my husband's family has always farmed foxes.

The men have always taught the boys
how to hammer together sheds
that house the long rows of cages
raised over the floor.
Fathers repeatedly caution how quickly foxes flee
to forest if a door is left unlatched.
Sons are shown how to feed them scraps
from fishermen's catch, and the ways
that they breed the silver and the red.

My youngest son's chore
is to rake the waste that falls though cages,
dredging the muck,
as vixens scurry above.

My husband and his hired hands
slaughter and skin the yearlings.
Our daughters and I stand in barns
where we can see our breath,
curing and tanning the pelts.

September aunts and uncles come to pack
the furs into trucks we drive through
the thousand and one tunnels from here
to Helsinki's fur market.

≈   ≈   ≈

In the blackness of the tunnels
I've never told my husband my imaginings —
animals flitting across the sweating walls
lit by our passing headlamps — a herd
of aurochs, a disturbed bear,
or perhaps we're about to blunder
into Grendel's mother's lair!

The deeper we drive into the marrow
of a mountain the more I'm full of fear —
that tunnel lamps will fail and we'll smash
into a runaway logging truck,
or be swallowed down to the mineral core.

Sometimes tunnels go on so long
my brain is tricked into night.
Again I am sleepless, walking late
beside the long, low sheds,
listening to vixens
nervously circling their cages,
their quick barks.

To myself I cry for the foxes.
I dream their cages fly open
and they escape to the woods.
But they return to burrow
into our walls, digging their den
just the other side of the bed
where I lie with my husband.
Their kits scrabble and mew me awake.

Then I grow afraid for our children,
afraid that Norway will tip into
eternal winter. I fear the cold
no number of furs can keep us from.

> *She ran with the heart of a locomotive,*
> *on champagne glass ankles — Sally Jenkins*

A big bruise of low pressure
moves across the TV's weather map.
The bottom ticker scrolls
breaking Derby news:

... The runner-up, Eight Belles, collapsed after the finish with
fractured ankles. She was euthanized on the track as Big
Brown was led into the Winner's Circle ...

What the forecaster calls
"the barometer falling through the floor"
is the ache in my right knee
or lament for a horse.

Once, lame horses were "put down"
with a gun. At Churchill Downs,
Eight Belles died from lethal injection.

... racehorses bred for big muscles and lightweight bones ...

≈   ≈   ≈

I dream I am still awake, afraid,
as a hungry ghost prowls downstairs,
tipping over the parlor palm,
upending chairs.

In the morning the malignant wind
has exhausted itself.
But Eight Belles runs on.

Off at the chimes the filly dashes, bandaged ankles, blinders,
man on her back flogging her flanks ...

In the replay once more they show
where her ankles break.

... She passes Denis of Cork, crosses second ...

APES IN SPACE AT THE SMITHSONIAN

Grainy news clips on a loop in a darkened room
of those first manned flights—
clumsy contraptions lumbering over dunes

barely airborne—more like chimps
swinging through trees
than a rising above our sphere.

But flying machines were soon climbing
into the firmament to drop fire,
to break sound's barrier.

Restless to escape gravity's cage,
we dispatched test-flight monkeys to breach
the black vacuum, eyeing the banana moon

before they perished from heat stroke,
or suffocation, explosion,
or failure of their parachutes.

Mummified under glass, Able
the rhesus is displayed, first ape
to survive the return to our world.

MAN LEADS WHOOPING CRANES
THROUGH LOST MIGRATION ROUTE

Year of the Housefly, spring of unhatching,
plummet of the census of the bird,
ancestral flyways forgotten.

All nines rolling over to zeroes
when Kent Clegg clucks to his brood
of whooping cranes

who follow his ultralight airplane
with black-tipped wings like theirs
up into the blue.

With his compass and maps
and his ground crew in vans below,
he is teaching the birds

what they didn't know they knew.
The last one had nearly been bagged
and tossed on the heap

of lapsed memory
when we turn, goggle-eyed,
to witness their flight over highway,

the plane in the lead with six birds
trailing in formation.
We had nearly added them

to our list of ignorance
when they arrive at the refuge,
wings spread wide, stepping out of the sky.

"The Black Madonna" — The Cathédral St. Jacques in Jacmel, Haiti, withstood the severe 2010 earthquake, though its clock was stopped.

"Explain to Me about Plums" — The epigraph is a refrain in Pablo Neruda's poem, "I Explain Some Things," and can be translated, "Come and see the blood in the streets."

"As the President Rallies the Nation" is dedicated to David Ther.

"Words from the Woods" — The epigraph is from an interview with the Israeli writer in *Poets & Writers*. The opening image was appropriated from the film *I Served the King of England* with screenplay by Jiří Menzel and based on the novel by Bohumil Hrabal.

"The Other Half" — Accounts of ordinary citizens' lives disrupted by land mine explosions are found in Philip C. Winslow's *Sowing the Dragon's Teeth*.

"Views of a Drone Pilot" — The poem is based on an interview in Dan Klaidman's *Kill or Capture: The War on Terror and the Soul of the Obama Presidency*.

"The Water Leveling with Us" — The penultimate line refers to massive accumulations of plastic debris in the oceans as documented by the National Oceanic and Atmospheric Administration at: http://marinedebris .noaa.gov/info/patch.html.

"Lines Written under 13,000 Pounds per Square Inch" —
The figure in the title is the estimated pressure with
which oil from the ruptured well was flowing into the
Gulf of Mexico. The closing stanzas refer to the symbolic
costume worn by participants in the late 19th century
Ghost Dance movement.

"Prepare" — This poem is dedicated to Joel Dailey.

"What We Last Saw" — This poem takes its cue from
José Saramago's *Blindness*.

"Late Spring Twilight" — This was written after reading
Tiffany Trent's "Midas's Turtle" in *Orion*.

"Nightmare after Eight Belles" — The filly named Eight
Belles broke both front ankles in taking second place in
the 2008 Kentucky Derby and was promptly killed by
lethal injection.

"Man Leads Whooping Cranes through Lost Migration
Route" — This poem is drawn from Kent Clegg's project
diary. Having imprinted whooping crane chicks on
himself, Clegg piloted an ultralight attempting to restore
their ancestral migration route from Grace, Idaho, to the
Bosque del Apache refuge in New Mexico.

ACKNOWLEDGEMENTS

Denise Low provided helpful comments on an early manuscript of this book. Also, my gratitude is due to Stephen Bunch, Sheila Cowing, Susan Gardner, Robyn Hunt, Wayne Lee, David Markwardt, Gary Moody, Mary Morris, Robert Ricci, Barbara Rockman, and Jane Shoenfeld for their insights on several of the poems. Working with Red Mountain Press has been an ideal author's experience.

Former NEA Fellow Donald Levering was born in Kansas City and received his MFA from Bowling Green (Ohio) State University. He has worked a teacher on the Navajo reservation, groundskeeper, and human services administrator. Featured in the Academy of American Poets Forum, the Ad Astra Poetry Project, and the Duende Series, he won the Quest for Peace Prize in rhetoric. Among his recent honors are finalist for both the Janet B. McCabe Prize and the Jane Kenyon Award. His poems have appeared in *The Alembic, Atlanta Review, Blue Rock Review, Bloomsbury Review, Columbia, Commonweal, Harpur Palate, Hiram Poetry Review, Hunger Mountain, Poet & Critic, Poet Lore, Quiddity, Southern Poetry Review, Water~Stone Review,* and *Yemassee.* He has published 11 books of poetry, most recently *Algonquins Planted Salmon* and *The Number of Names.* A father of two children, he is married to the artist Jane Shoenfeld and lives in Santa Fe, New Mexico, where he is a species preservation (great white shark, leatherback turtle, queen conch) and human rights activist. Visit him at donaldlevering.com.

The Water Leveling With Us is set in Palatino,
a 20th century font designed by Hermann Zapf
based on the humanist typefaces of the Italian
Renaissance and named for the 16th century
Italian master of calligraphy Giambattista Palatino.